Reptile Keeper's Guides

CORN SNAKES

R.D. Bartlett
Patricia Bartlett

BARRON'S

Acknowledgments

Throughout the years we have met many corn snake
enthusiasts and have learned from all. In particular we
would like to thank RobRoy MacInnes, Bill and Kathy Love,
Bill and Marcia Brant, Rich and Connie Zuchowski, Travis
Cossette, Doug Kranich, Jake Scott, and John Decker.

All inquiries should be addressed to:
Barron's Educational Series, Inc.
250 Wireless Boulevard
Hauppauge, NY 11788
www.barronseduc.com

Library of Congress Control Number: 2011008191

ISBN: 978-0-7641-4610-7

Library of Congress Cataloging-in-Publication Data

Bartlett, Richard D., 1938–
    Corn snakes / R.D. Bartlett, Patricia Bartlett. — 2nd ed.
      p. cm. — (Reptile keeper's guides)
    Includes bibliographical references and index.
    ISBN 978-0-7641-4610-7 (pbk.)
    1. Corn snakes as pets. I. Bartlett, Patricia Pope, 1949–
II. Title.
SF409.55.B27 2011
639.3'96—dc22   2011008191

Printed in China
9 8 7 6 5 4 3 2 1

Contents

What Is a Corn Snake?
2

The "Other" Corn Snakes
6

The Corn Snake As a Pet
9

Colors and Morphs
14

Caging
26

Feeding
30

Health
32

Breeding
38

Glossary
44

Helpful Information
46

Index
46

What Is a Corn Snake?

The corn snake is a brightly colored, constricting snake species found in the eastern United States. In the wild, it is found in varied habitats from wood lots and rocky hillsides to agricultural land and brushy roadsides. It inhabits a large range from western Louisiana northward and eastward to southeastern Tennessee and the Pine Barrens of New Jersey and then southward to the tip of the Florida Keys. Disjunct colonies exist in central and northeast Kentucky.

Corn snakes are colubrids (family Colubridae), a nonvenomous group that includes about 78 percent of all the snake species in the world. In North America, the vast majority of snakes (85 percent of the genera) are colubrids. Examples of other colubrids are king snakes, milk snakes, and garter snakes.

The corn snake is an adept climber but is basically a terrestrial species. It can often be found under human-generated surface debris such as sheets of tin or plywood. The belly scales (or scutes) are angled at both sides, an adaptation to help with climbing. The scaly skin is dry to the touch. In fact, the scales are formed of intricately folded areas of skin.

The corn snake, *Elaphe guttata guttata*, is also known as the red rat snake. Both of its common names refer to where it can be found (in corn cribs or near corn fields) and to its prey. About a half-dozen other rat snakes live in the United States, such as the fox snake and the black, yellow, and gray rat snakes. However, only the corn snake bears the distinctive black-bordered red blotches on a noticeably lighter background and also a spear

Despite their bright colors, corn snakes blend remarkably well with old stumps and pine needles.

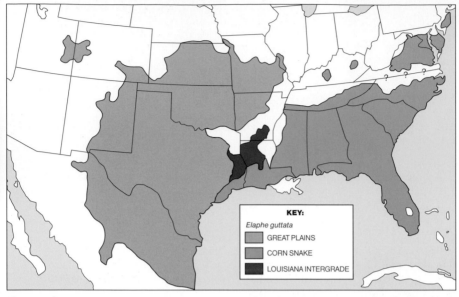

Corn snake range map.

KEY:
Elaphe guttata
GREAT PLAINS
CORN SNAKE
LOUISIANA INTERGRADE

point design on the top of its head. In the west, the corn snake's closest relative is the Great Plains rat snake, *Elaphe guttata emoryi*. They differ only in color; the Great Plains race has a much drabber brown-on-gray coloration. Where their ranges overlap, these subspecies may interbreed.

At one time, the corn snakes of the Florida Keys, referred to as rosy rat snakes by hobbyists, were also considered a separate subspecies. They were designated as *Elaphe guttata rosacea*. A classic rosy displayed a pale orange ground color, pastel red saddles, and reduced black pigment. Although this is no longer a valid race, hobbyists continue to differentiate the Keys corn snakes from those of the mainland.

The corn snake is an oviparous (egglaying) species. Healthy wild females often lay up to 20 (usually fewer but sometimes more) eggs in a clutch. They may produce a second

This pretty orange-hued corn snake was found on Florida's western panhandle.

clutch later in the season. Healthy captive females lay from 12 to 25 eggs in the first clutch of the year, routinely double clutch, and may rarely triple clutch (see the chapter on breeding for more information).

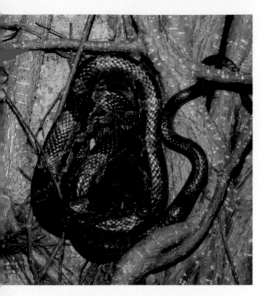

In some regions corn snakes readily ascend palms and other easy-to-climb trees.

The adult size of corn snakes varies. Many specimens from the Florida Keys and the adjacent mainland attain a length of only 28 to 36 inches (11 to 91 cm). Those from the northern part of the range may grow to 49 to 54 inches (124 to 137 cm). The greatest authenticated length to date is 72 inches (183 cm). When hatched, corn snakes measure between 8 to 11 inches (20 to 28 cm) in length.

These snakes usually adapt well to captivity. In fact, most of those now offered for sale are themselves descendants of generations of captivity. As a result of this almost-domestication—and partly due to the calm nature of the snake—corn snakes are easy to maintain and to breed. As adults, captive corn snakes thrive on rodent prey. Most hatchlings and virtually all juveniles do likewise. Most pet stores sell frozen mice and rats, which can be simply warmed to about 95°F (35°C) in warm water and blotted dry before feeding them to your corn snake. In the wild, hatchling corn snakes may also feed on amphibians and small lizards. Corn snakes from extreme south Florida may prefer lizards (including the introduced brown anole). This could be due to an avail-

Crimson to strawberry red saddles on a stark white ground color typify the candy cane corn snake.

ability factor. An occasional hatchling may insist on eating lizards or tree frogs at the beginning. These hold-outs can usually be switched to a diet of pinky mice within a few meals by scenting the pinky (see page 30).

Distinctive Adaptations

All snake species have their own unique characteristics, yet they share many common characteristics. Although they do not possess an external ear, they can hear. Their auditory apparatus consists of a quadrate bone, which is attached to a jawbone rather than to a tympanum or ear drum. In effect, their jawbone is the sound-gathering device. Snakes can hear low-frequency sounds well and react to ground vibrations with alacrity.

Snakes have no eyelids. However, the eyes of most are protected by a *brille*, a single transparent scale. Their vision is especially attuned to detecting motion. The brille is shed and replaced as part of the shedding process.

When their vision is combined with their sense of smell, snakes are adept at finding food and evading predators. The tongue is used to pick up molecules of scent. It then transfers those molecules to the Jacobson's organ in the palate. Analysis of the molecules is remarkably acute. The odors of food animals, potential predators, and pheromones (breeding-readiness hormones) are readily discerned.

Prey items are swallowed whole, and elasticity in the snake's jaws allows comparatively large prey to be swallowed. First one side of the

A natural striping that is most visible when the snake is entering its shed cycle is known among some populations of corn snakes along Florida's east coast.

mouth, then the other, advances and withdraws, engaging the recurved teeth and drawing the prey down the throat. Throat contractions then propel the prey into the stomach.

Compared with the lizards, from which they evolved, snakes are comparative newcomers to our world. Scientists believe that snakes first appeared during the Cretaceous period. This last period of the Mesozoic era occurred about 140 million years ago.

The serpentine form seems to have worked well for snakes. The attenuated body shape requires some changes in paired organs. In corn snakes, the left lung is small, while the right lung is well developed and fully functional. The disadvantage is that with only a single working lung, respiratory problems in corn snakes are especially serious.

The "Other" Corn Snakes

Of the four snakes discussed here, two are and two are not related to *Pantherophis guttatus*.

We will first discuss the two related forms, the Great Plains rat snake and the "Louisiana" corn snake.

The Great Plains rat snake, *Pantherophis guttatus emoryi*, is listed by some researchers as a full species having the name *Pantherophis emoryi*. This westerly form of the corn snake ranges widely from central-western Illinois southward well into Mexico, and westward to Colorado, Utah, and New Mexico.

Obviously a corn snake in pattern, rather than having saddles and lateral spots hued in red or orange, the saddles of the Great Plains rat snake are tan, reddish-brown, brown, brownish-gray, or gray. The belly is usually strongly checkerboarded, but in some populations may lack all patterning. Somewhat smaller than the corn snake, the record size of the Great Plains rat snake is only 62 inches. Most examples are adult at four feet or less in length. Drawn by the presence of small rodents and lizards, the Great Plains rat snake may be abundant in agricultural and suburban locales.

The snake now occasionally designated as the Louisiana corn snake, *P. g. slowinskii*, was long considered an intergrade between the easterly corn snake and the westerly Great Plains rat snake. We (and many researchers) continue to consider it an intergrade. Adults of this snake bear dark-edged chocolate saddles against a muddy ground color, while the hatchlings are dark gray on light gray. A strong iridescence often plays over the scales. This intergrade form ranges over much of Louisiana, adjacent Arkansas, and extreme eastern Texas. Like most corn snakes they are easily maintained, and even wild-collected examples will usually accept pre-killed lab mice. This dark-colored snake is occasionally available in the pet trade. Examples from the eastern part of the range

This subtly colored Great Plains rat snake is from east Texas.

tend to be a bit larger than those from East Texas.

In one or the other of its three subspecies, the Mexican night snake, *Pseudelaphe flavirufa*, ranges southward from northeastern Mexico to northern Central America. Formerly referred to as the Mexican corn snake, an attempt is being made to standardize the common name of this nocturnal serpent as "Mexican night snake." Unless locality information is available (and it seldom is), it is very difficult to differentiate the two most common and colorful of the subspecies, the Mexican, *P. f. flavirufa*, and the Central American, *P. f. pardalina*. This pretty snake is adult at from 36 to about 60 inches in length, but most adults seen measure between 40 and 50 inches in length. The dorsal color consists of black-edged, irregular maroon blotches, saddles, or broad zigzag striping on a ground color of gray. A row of small, black-edged maroon spots runs along each side. The belly is light with dark spots along the sides of some ventral scutes. The sutures of the large

The deep hues of the corn snakes from Louisiana allow for a wonderful iridescence.

head scales are dark, giving the head a sculptured look. The eyes are large, bluish or grayish-white, with small round pupils. An anerythristic strain has been developed; on these the red is replaced by grays and charcoals. Mexican night snakes will usually readily accept pre-killed lab rodents.

The Eurasian leopard rat snake, *Zamenis situla*, is a smaller corn snake look-alike. It is fully adult at up to 36 inches in length, but rarely longer than 28 to 30 inches. Its belly is predominantly black, with many ventral scutes

Deep red to chocolate saddles against a brownish ground color are typical of the Louisiana corn snakes. These are referred to by some as *P. g. slowinskii*.

Pseudelaphe flavirufa is variously known as the Mexican corn snake or the Mexican night snake. The latter name accurately describes this snake's nocturnal lifestyle. It is now captive bred in normal and anerythristic color morphs.

bearing a small white spot along each outer edge. Above each white spot a black triangle extends upward for two scale rows. The ground color is a warm tan. Black-outlined dorsal markings, whether saddles, spots, stripes, bars, or combinations, are usually a deep rose. There is a row of small black spots along each side. The face, some upper labial scales, the suture between the parietal plates, and the rostral scale are patterned with black bars.

Now that captive-bred babies have become available to hobbyists, the leopard rat snake is finally overcoming its reputation of being a difficult captive. While it is true that many wild-collected examples were steadfast in their refusal to accept laboratory mice (insisting on white-footed mice

or voles as prey), most of today's captive-bred babies will readily accept small lab mice. However, make certain the leopard snake you are interested in purchasing does feed.

Like the corn snake, these four rat snakes are well able to climb, but are predominantly terrestrial.

In most cases, to stimulate captive breeding these four rat snakes will require a 60- to 90-day period of winter cooling. A temperature of 56–62°F is suggested. During this period a reduced photoperiod or complete darkness should be provided. At all times, both during periods of normal activity and cooling, fresh water should be provided. If you do not intend to breed your snakes, they may be kept warm, active, and illuminated throughout the year. Please refer to pages 40–41 for additional suggestions on the safe winter cooling of your snakes.

The Eurasian leopard rat snake, *Zamenis situla*, is a corn snake look-alike. It occurs naturally in both a saddled and a striped morph.

The Corn Snake As a Pet

You can obtain a corn snake in several straightforward ways. Most people purchase one. You can certainly catch your own, but that may take more time and money than buying one.

The simplest way is to call your area pet stores until you locate one or more that has corn snakes in stock. While on the phone, ask if the animal is an adult or a hatchling and if it is a male or a female. Male and female corn snakes do not exhibit any behavioral or temperamental differences. However, in case you ever want to breed your snake, you'll need to know what you have. Ask also if the snake is feeding and if it is a normally colored corn snake or if it is a color morph (see the next chapter for descriptions of the various color morphs).

If you decide to buy a hatchling, remember that you will need to find a supplier of pinky mice for food; however, you should be aware that some baby corn snakes (and even a very occasional larger specimen) are problematic feeders, and that fussiness is usually directly related to the corn morph. Baby corn snakes of the blood red phase may refuse food entirely. Inducing feeding in some other color phases can be difficult. This is true for those from the Lower Florida Keys. Miami phase corns may insist on anole lizards or house geckos for their first few meals. For these, you will need to provide the correct prey before you begin to offer scented pinky mice (see page 30 for details on scenting). Be certain the snake you choose is eating.

Although the vast majority of pet shops strive to provide all the services and the best animals possible, your shop simply cannot control some factors. Your pet shop may not know the origin of a given wild-collected specimen or the genetics of either a normal-appearing, or a color morph. Remember, the pet shop is often two or even three or four times removed from the initial dealing that placed the specimen into the pet trade.

This pretty Miami phase corn snake bears just a tinge of orange in the gray interspaces.

Butter yellow corn snakes were developed in the late 1990s.

If your local pet shops do not carry corn snakes or if you would like to buy one of the more unusual color morphs, you may want to try one of the specialty dealers or a breeder who will sell to the retail trade. Besides often producing fair numbers of the reptiles they offer, specialty dealers deal directly with other breeders across the world. In this way, they often cut out one or two levels of intermediaries and are in a better position to provide you with more accurate answers to many of your questions. Their imported specimens are usually acclimated,

have been fed, and have often been subjected to a veterinary checkup. The broadest selection of corn snake colors are usually available from the specialty dealers.

Herp expos are a great way to see and obtain different color morphs of corn snakes. Expos allow both new and experienced hobbyists to meet the breeders and importers of the animals in which they are interested. Hobbyists can ask questions about, as well as see, the actual specimens. Reptile shows and expos are an effective, but not necessarily the most inexpensive, method of acquiring reptiles. Shows are usually advertised in the reptile and amphibian magazines.

Breeders are another good source of parasite-free, well-acclimated specimens and accurate information. These breeders can be backroom hobbyists who specialize in just one species (or even a single subspecies) or commercial breeders who literally produce thousands of baby snakes a year for the pet trade. Many breeders keep records of genetics, lineage, fecundity,

This prettily marked corn snake was found in Collier County, Florida.

health, or quirks of the specimens with which they work. These records are invariably available to the purchasers of offspring. Chances are that good records will leave very few questions unanswered.

Collecting Your Own Corn Snake from the Wild

Corn snakes, and all other herpeto-fauna, are protected by some states but may be legally collected in others. If you want to collect your own corn snake, get permission before you go onto private land, and do not hunt in state or federal parks.

To hunt for corn snakes, look at the edges of old agricultural fields (corn and soybean fields are favored), at woodland edges (especially those where litter is strewn about), or even in urban areas where some cover such as fallen logs or pieces of plywood can be found. In the early spring, walk slowly along the field and woodland edges, and turn debris (especially roofing tins or other such cover). Many people use a snake stick to turn logs, rocks, or tin. Be careful and cautious. Venomous snakes also seek such cover. If you do come across a venomous snake species, just carefully replace the tin or cover, move a short distance away, and resume searching.

When the weather is warm, drive slowly along old country roads in the early evening. Corn snakes often cross these, especially on spring evenings. Again, be certain you know what you are picking up before you pick it up! Corns are not the only snakes that cross roadways.

Few things are more beautiful than the sight of your first corn snake in the wild. Its colors seem to glow against the background. If you're certain you're looking at a corn snake, simply reach down and pick it up.

What if it bites you? We've picked up many corn snakes in the wild and have been bitten only a few times. Corn snakes tend to let go after biting. If your snake fails to turn you loose, put your hand with the snake into a cloth snake bag. It should release you and seek safety in the bag. Or try lowering your hand to the ground and releasing it (temporarily). Wash the bitten area with soap and water and keep it dry and clean until the bite marks close up.

Once you have the snake in hand, place it into a snake bag or pillowcase, twist the neck of the bag to seal it, and tie it into a knot. Keep the bag and its contents away from direct sunlight and at temperatures between 75 and 85°F (24 and 29°C) until you can place the snake into its new cage.

Prairie rat snakes, *Pantherophis guttatus emoryi*, are gray to tan and in most populations have strongly checkered bellies.

Corn snakes of both normal and designer colors have become so readily available that many choices are often available in local pet and reptile stores. But as you advance in your hobby, there is always that one newly developed color or pattern variant that is available only on the opposite side of the country from you. Getting the desired snake from point A to point B could be perplexing, but it's very do-able.

Several door-to-door shipping and delivery companies will whisk the snake from breeder to purchaser in a matter of hours. They have firm packaging regulations for reptiles, so find out what they are. The actual shipping cost varies by distance, value of the package, and the size and weight of the shipping box, but is usually between $35 and $60.

Shippers are familiar with the procedures required by the door-to-door carriers, but remember that adverse weather conditions might be encountered by the carrier and make shipping at a given time inadvisable. Always consider the weather conditions—extreme cold, extreme heat, impending storms, or other conditions that might cause the cancellation or delay of flights—at not only the points of origin and destination, but at transfer points as well. Adverse ramp temperatures at a transfer point can quickly alter the temperature in even an insulated shipping box. Your supplier will probably have 48-hour heat packs or cold packs available. These will make shipping during questionable weather conditions safer. Discuss live delivery guarantees with your shipper, for the carriers are reluctant to accept responsibility. This is especially so when weather-related or mechanical delays occur.

In this digital age, most suppliers will be happy to e-mail you a photograph of the actual corn snake you are purchasing. Most require payment in full before they will ship. This will include the cost of the corn snake(s), packing supplies, and shipping charges. For that reason it is important that you check the honesty and integrity of your supplier. A big name in the business might well indicate integrity, or it may not. COD service may be available but the terms of service will make this service more expensive and often inconvenient.

Unless you are known to the carrier and have a signature on file it is important that you be home to sign for, accept, and inspect your arriving snake. Failure to be available will often negate any live arrival guarantees that your supplier provides. Most priority shipments are delivered before noon, but flight delays may delay delivery time.

A corn snake from Glades County, Florida.

On the very rare occasion that a corn snake does die in transit, it is probable that your supplier will want a digital photo as proof, sent to them by e-mail within a prespecified length of time. This type of documentation will also be necessary if you find any other discrepancies.

In the event that you and your shipper find airport-to-airport service more convenient, be certain that you furnish your supplier with the name of the destination airport you choose. This is especially important if you live in or near a city that is serviced by more than a single airport.

Colors and Morphs

In the 1940s, a corn snake was a corn snake. Those from the Pine Barrens of New Jersey or from the southern tip of the Florida mainland differed somewhat in color than those from South Carolina. However, all were easily identifiable as the same species, a corn snake. When hobbyists found that corn snakes could be bred in captivity, the only goal was to supply the pet market with healthy, captive-bred hatchlings. Then a wild-caught albino turned up here, and a few anerythristics turned up there. Corn snake fanciers found they could actually breed for albinos; line breeding could produce more intensely colored Okeetees and paler Miami phases. They found that when various phases were bred together, new color morphs formed. The race of discovery was on.

Today, over thirty different colors and patterns are available. You cannot know what may be in the background of the normal-appearing corn snake you purchase. To give you a basic understanding about what has transpired, remember that every color morph displays in some combination reduced or increased pigment levels of black, red, or yellow—the three colors found in normal corn snakes. A color morph will also exhibit reduced or increased white—the color that results when all pigments are missing.

Three types of cells control the pigment in corn snakes. Melanophores control the amount of black. Xanthophores control the levels of red and yellow. Iridophores control the iridescence, the rainbow-like reflection that sometimes plays over the surface of a corn snake's body but that appears more obvious in snakes like the pythons.

When you begin to breed for a pattern as well as for color, the process grows more complex. However, we will deal with color first. (And of course, no matter what their color, captive corn snakes should not be released into the wild.)

At the outset of the captive breeding craze, breeding corn snakes for desired color or pattern traits was a simple matter. Breeding for a characteristic is called linebreeding. Most of the breeder snakes available were wild-collected specimens that carried few, if any, aberrant characteristics. If you wanted to breed for darker corn snakes, you could simply linebreed dark corn snakes to dark corn snakes and breed their darkest young to each other. Pretty soon you would end up with really dark corn snakes. If you wanted to breed for a recessive trait, simple Mendelian genetic principles applied. Today, though the same genetic principles apply, an entirely

different matter exists. After 25 years of color and pattern manipulation, corn snakes now carry an extensive hodgepodge of recessive color genes. Breeding similar-appearing specimens and having three or more entirely different color morphs appear in the progeny from that breeding is entirely possible.

To begin to understand the complexities involved, you will need to learn a little bit about genetics. Simply put, a snake is considered heterozygous for a trait if it carries both a dominant and a recessive gene or allele for the same trait. If the snake has both a dominant and a recessive allele, the dominant gene will mask the recessive. If the snake has two recessive alleles, the recessive coloration or trait will appear. We will use albinism (amelanism) as an example.

A corn snake heterozygous for albinism appears normal because the gene for normal coloration is dominant over (or masks) the gene for albinism. Breed two heterozygous snakes together, and the offspring will receive one allele for coloration from each parent. A Punnett square (named for the man who developed it) demonstrates the process. Each snake is heterozygous for albinism; the dominant gene for normal coloration (A) masks the albino gene (a):

Each parent contributes either a dominant (A) or recessive (a) gene for coloration. How these genes pair up in the young determines the color. One-quarter of the young will be homozygous for the normal coloration (AA) and appear normal in coloration. One-half will be heterozygous (Aa; the dominant gene is listed first) and will also appear normal in coloration. The remaining one-quarter of the young will be homozygous for albinism (aa) or albinos. You can tell which normal-appearing snakes bear which genes only by breeding two of them and seeing what their young look like.

Their young are called the F1 generation or first filial generation. If the parents have one dominant and one recessive gene for albinism, the F1 young will have the same mix as their parents' chart shown previously. If you breed a heterozygous snake and a homozygous dominant snake together, their young will look like this:

	A	a
A	AA	Aa
a	Aa	aa

	A	A
A	AA	AA
a	Aa	Aa

Normal

Before discussing these several forms, allow us to state that what is considered a normal corn snake will differ by what part of the country you are discussing. Corn snakes are found from the Pine Barrens of New Jersey to Kentucky and from those states southward to Louisiana and South Florida, and for the most part these are snakes bearing bright orange-red to red blotches with a narrow black edging on a ground color of orange. The orange ground may be a bit lighter on the sides than on the back. There is a row of dark, irregular, lateral spots along each side. There is usually a stylized spear point on the crown. The belly is strongly patterned with black and white.

Okeetee

Considered the most attractive of the naturally occurring phases, the Okeetee corn is abundant in the Low Country of the Carolinas and adjacent Georgia. The term Okeetee

refers to the hunt club of the same name in Jasper County, South Carolina. It was in his 1950s writings that herpetologist Carl Kauffeld first brought attention of this snake to what was then a very small herpetocultural community. Kauffeld remarked on the brilliance and contrast

This pretty corn snake was found foraging in early evening in a stand of Australian pines on Sugarloaf Key.

of colors on this snake, and his vivid description has become legend. Although not all corn snakes from that region are created equal in color, the phase most coveted has bright red blotches with wide black edging on a ground color of burnished orange. The belly is checkered with pale orange and black. The spear point on the crown is bright red. Occasional individuals having similar characteristics may occur elsewhere over the range of the corn snake.

Deep red saddles on a silvery gray background describes the "Miami phase" corn snake from Florida's southern peninsula.

Miami

On the southernmost tip of the Florida Peninsula, amidst the warehouse complexes, plowed-over fields, and oolitic limestone-edged driveways and gardens, you may encounter the red-saddled, silvery gray "Miami corn snake." While it is true that this color phase of the corn snake occurs in and around Miami, it actually ranges well to the south of that city. Amazingly resilient, this corn snake continues to thrive on the light-colored limestone substrates (where soils are darker, the corn snakes are also usually darker) amid the rubble-strewn vacant lots, canal banks, and other degraded habitat. This slender snake seems to feed preferentially upon the brown anoles now ubiquitous to the region. In fact, enticing the hatchlings to accept pink mice as their prey can be a challenge. The adult size is usually less than 36 inches. Gravid females of less than an 18-inch length have been found.

Anerythristic Type A and Type B (Axanthic)

In some areas of southwest and south-central Florida, Type A anerythristic corn snakes seem nearly as common as the normal ones. These snakes are also known as black albinos, seemingly a contradiction in terms.

The Type A anerythristics have a gray ground and well-defined, dark dorsal saddles and lateral blotches. The belly is a checkerboard of black and light gray. A dark spear point is on the crown. An elongate yellow wash that becomes more vivid with advancing age is present on each side of the neck.

Type B anerythristic corn snakes are much rarer in the wild, but captive-bred forms are readily available. They may be referred to as charcoals or Pine Island anerythristics. When compared to the Type A, the dorsal saddles of the adults of this genetic morph do not contrast as sharply with the ground color and may contain gray scales. If any yellow is present, it is restricted to the barest suffusion on each side of the neck immediately posterior to the head. The spear point on the head may or may not be visible. In overall appearance this snake is very reminiscent of a gray rat snake.

Unlike many color aberrancies (such as albinism) that render a snake more visible and therefore more subject to predation, the darkening caused by anerythrism may work to the snake's advantage, lessening its visibility.

A portrait of an anerythristic corn snake.

Not all Okeetee phase corn snakes are as intensely colored as this example.

The overwash of orange on the sides provides a bit of color for this pale ghost corn snake.

All the young will appear normal, but half of them will bear the gene for albinism. If you breed two corn snakes that are Aa for albinism, a quarter of their offspring will be albinos.

If you breed two albinos together, you will be breeding what is called double recessives (each parent can contribute only the recessive gene for albinism). Those offspring will all be albinos, because no dominant genes are in their gene pool.

As you can tell, keeping accurate records of the genetics of each snake you produce is critical to predicting the results of any future breeding. You may have to breed corn snakes for several generations before you acquire enough albino (or any other recessive trait) stock to produce nothing but albinos.

When breeding for albinism began, we thought that just one type of albinism existed—a snake lacking black pigment and having pink eyes. That type of albinism is a simple dominant/recessive allele. Now we know that different types of albinism exist—complete albinos, partial albinos, albinism that affects only spe-cific regions of the snake's body (like a piebald corn snake), and genetic defect albinos. (This last type of albino possesses nonfunctional melanophores, the cells that form dark pigment. One type, Type B amelanistic, lacks tyrosinase, the enzyme that permits the formation of melanin. The second type, Type A amelanistic, has a tyrosinase inhibitor that prohibits the passage of tyrosine, a melanin precursor, into the melanophore).

Natural or Derived

In its natural form, the corn snake is readily recognizable. It is when a hobbyist is contemplating the many breeder-originated names for the various designer color phases (or morphs) that confusion may arise. You will find that numerous corn snake morphs of similar appearance have different names. In some cases, this is because designer corn snakes

A beautiful adult red-albino (sunglow phase) corn snake.

of similar appearance may have a very different genetic background. In other cases, it is simply a case of an identical snake being named differently by the breeders who produced them. We can offer no solution for this, except to recommend that if you are looking for a corn snake of a specific color and a specific genetic background, find a supplier that you can trust.

Dark red ground and blotch color with little outlining is typical of corn snakes in some northeastern Florida populations.

Colors

Albino (Amelanistic)

A fair number of albino corn snakes have been found in the wild. Selective breeding provides those in the pet market. Several phases and as many names are involved here. Casual hobbyists usually just refer to the amelanistic corn snakes as "albinos." Depending on a number of variables, this pink-eyed color morph may be white with crimson saddles (candy cane) or orange with bright orange-red saddles. The saddles may (fluorescent orange corn) or may not (sunglow corn) have a narrow white edging.

Northeast Florida (Hastings)

These corns, found from northeastern Alachua County to western Duval County, are the snakes from which the blood red morph was derived. The wild examples are among the reddest of the corn snakes. The body color is red, the saddles (which are either narrowly edged in black or unedged) are a darker red, and the belly is a paler red, blotched with white. The spear point on the crown is pale and may be just barely visible. Hatchlings are paler, being quite like the normal corn snake in color and pattern contrast.

Florida Keys Variants

If you continue to drive southward from the mainland of Florida, you will travel Highway US-1 along the loose crescent of tiny island and islets known as the Florida Keys. The Keys stretch over 100 miles of shallow water with Key Largo at the north and Key West at the south. For much of that measured distance you are in the

realm of the snake once known as the rosy rat snake and designated scientifically as *Elaphe guttata rosacea*. Today it is just considered a corn snake, and a relatively obscure morph at that. This corn snake lives in mangrove strands and elevated hammock habitats, as well as in tree lines and on pine-palmetto highlands.

The name of rosy rat snake did not do justice to the Keys snake, for it actually comes in a variety of colors, rosy being only one of them. In addition to the rosy phase, there are olive, silver, and orange phases and a strange phase that has chocolate saddles when young but which matures into a typical orange phase adult. No matter the ground and saddle color, the corn snakes of the Florida Keys were typified by a dramatic reduction in the amount of visible black pigment (melanin). In the lingo of today's herpetoculturists, these Keys snakes border on the verge of being hypomelanistic. Additionally, they are adult at from 22 to 28 inches in total length. In fact, they seldom exceed 30 inches in length and are of proportionately slender build.

The rosy phase tends to be just that, a grayish snake with rose pink saddles. (Many corn snakes of the Tampa Bay region are similar to this in color but attain a larger size.)

The orange phase is grayish to tan, with saddles that are definitely on the orange side of rose.

The olive phase has a grayish or tan ground color, orangish saddles, and a pale olive suffusion over all.

The silver phase of the Keys is very like the silvery examples of the Miami phase corn snakes of the mainland.

The term "chocolate phase" only fits some juveniles. The body is grayish

This silver phase corn snake is from the Florida Keys.

and the saddles are brownish red. At maturity it is identical to the orange phase.

Most hatchlings and many adults of the Florida Keys variant will accept lizards as prey more readily than they will rodents.

It seems that the Keys corn snakes of the Lower Keys are paler and lack more melanin than those of the Upper Keys. However, it should be noted that this species is protected in the Lower Keys.

This Florida Keys corn snake was found sunning on a low palm frond.

Natural Striping

Again, this is a self-defining but not often seen term. Some populations of the corn snake have four rather well-defined dark stripes that are especially visible when the snake is entering the shed cycle. This characteristic is often seen in corn snakes from southern Duval to Palm Beach County, Florida (see photo on page 5).

Selectively Derived Colors

Blood Red

This, the reddest of the corn snake morphs, is the result of selective breeding of the Northeastern Florida (Hastings) corn snake. The well-developed dorsal saddles of the hatchlings are soon obscured by the increased red pigment. Dorsal and lateral surfaces become a rich red in color and the belly is a bit paler, often with some white blotching. The dorsal saddles may be just a bit darker than the ground color but often are not.

The saddles are not outlined by black pigment. The spear point on the head is obscured. Striped blood-red corns have been developed.

Crimson

This is a hypomelanistic Miami phase corn snake. The dorsal saddles are a bright reddish-orange, the ground color is nearly white (a very pale red blush is often present dorsally), and the spear point on the head is well developed.

Candy Cane

At its best, this is a beautiful stark white and coral red to crimson corn snake. However, as these snakes age, many develop a variably defined suffusion of yellow or orange on the body. This is usually most visible on the sides of the neck.

Snow

The snow corn was created by crossing an amelanistic variant with an anerythristic. The ground color is white. The blotches of the adults may be pale pink, yellow, or green. A yellow wash is present on the sides of the neck and may also suffuse the throat.

Blood-red corns may or may not have visible saddles.

This juvenile snow-motley corn snake may become even paler as it matures.

Reverse Okeetee

In this case the name can be very misleading. Rather than hailing from the Low Country of South Carolina as the true Okeetee phase does, the Reverse Okeetee corn snake may be based on any brightly colored corn snake having the saddles strongly outlined in black. The black saddle edging is replaced by white and the black belly markings are replaced by pale orange.

Blizzard

Blizzards are pure white with red eyes. Vague saddling may be visible on some examples. This remarkable corn snake was the result of breeding an amelanistic (albino) corn snake with a Type B anerythristic corn snake.

Ghost

Although this term might lead you to think that this phase is bland and unexciting, this is not the case at all. This variant is the result of a hypomelanistic corn snake being bred to a Type A anerythristic corn snake.

Lavender

This pale purple-blotched, pinkish corn snake can be quite similar to a ghost in overall appearance.

Caramel

This is an interesting but variably colored corn snake. The yellowish ground color is often suffused with a brown patina. The saddles may vary from yellowish brown to a rich seal brown, and the saddles often darken as the snake ages.

Hypomelanistic (or Hypo)

The prefix "hypo" indicates that this morph has a reduced amount

The markings on a blizzard phase corn snake are so faint as to be almost imagined.

of melanin (black pigment). This trait is observable in corn snakes of many colors; thus you may see a hypo caramel or a hypo normal corn.

Christmas

This red on red corn snake was developed by The Gourmet Rodent. The red saddles are edged in forest green rather than in black.

Pepper (Pewter)

This charcoal corn snake has a diffused pattern, which results in poorly

Although other phases may actually be paler, the ghost corn snake (pictured) was among the first of these reduced-contrast beauties.

This is a pretty juvenile striped albino corn snake.

defined blotches that do not contrast sharply with the ground color.

Butter

Derived from the pairing of an amelanistic corn with a caramel corn, the butter corn snake has a warm yellow ground color and richer yellow dorsal saddles and lateral spots. Scattered white markings may be present on the dorsum. The belly is yellow and white. Depending on the genetics involved, besides the normally patterned phase, motley and striped variants are also available. The descriptive name of gold dust corn may be given to some of the more golden-yellow examples. These may have scattered grayish (rather than white) markings.

Opal

In overall appearance this color variant is similar to a blizzard corn but adds in an opalescent sheen.

Amber

This coloration was derived by breeding a hypomelanistic corn snake with a caramel. The ground color is pale brown and the saddles are amber.

Selectively Derived Patterns

Diffused

Rather than a color or pattern, this term is used when precise pattern delineation is obscured genetically. As an example, the edges of the dorsal saddles and later spots become softened and irregular. Additionally, the belly pattern is obscured or eliminated.

Genetic Striping

In the best examples, the two dorsolateral and two lateral stripes are complete, or nearly so. Some saddling may be vaguely visible. The ground color may be normal or amelanistic. Striping against other ground colors is being developed.

Zigzag

This is a snake with dorsal blotches arranged in a zigzag pattern. Normal, amelanistic, and other colors are available.

Aztec

Although an irregular pattern, the dorsal markings are well defined.

With blotches, stripes, and zigzags, the Aztec pattern is confusingly asymmetrical.

24

They may consist of a vertebral stripe, saddles, broken stripes, and zigzags. The Aztec pattern is available in normal and amelanistic phases.

Milk Snake

This corn snake has been selectively bred to have the dorsal saddles extended into bars that reach down the sides and may or may not incorporate at least some of the lateral blotches. Any given bar may reach the ventral scutes on both sides.

Motley

The dark patterning of this variant seems best defined as any pattern (combinations of dorsal ocelli, saddles, striping, and/or zigzag patterns, usually in combinations) that cannot be otherwise classified.

Intergrade Color Anomaly

Creamsicle (Normal and Striped)

This enticing name applies to an amelanistic intergrade between the easterly corn snake and its western relative, the Great Plains rat snake. This pretty designer snake has either blotches or stripes of "popsicle orange" against a ground color of "creamsicle white." Rather dull as a hatchling, the oranges intensify with age and growth.

Root Beer

If the genes for albinism are not factored in, the resulting snake is usually brighter than a Great Plains rat but duller than a corn snake. Certain normal intergrades can produce a snake that looks very much like the Louisiana corn snake.

Cinnamon

This is the hypomelanistic expression of the intergrading of a normally colored corn snake and Great Plains rat snake.

Intergeneric Hybrids

Jungle Corns

This name has been given to the progeny produced when a corn snake is bred to a California kingsnake. Physically, the progeny may look more like a kingsnake than a corn, or vice versa. Similarly, the markings may resemble those of one parent or the other or be intermediate.

Corn snakes may also be hybridized with various milk snakes. Confusing patterns (and catchy names) are then the norm. Do not confuse these corn snake—milk snake hybrids with the milk snake phase of the corn snake.

Striping is now well developed in the creamsicle corn snake. This hobbyist favorite is actually an intergrade between the corn snake and the Great Plains rat snake.

Caging

A cage for your corn snake can be simple, or it can be ornate. The choice is determined by your budget, physical space, and alloted maintenance time. Cage choices range from a large plastic blanket box set up with a newspaper substrate, a water bowl, and a hiding area to complex, custom-made, naturalistic terraria. We will discuss easy-to-use caging in this book.

The Enclosure

Whether a glass aquarium, plastic shoe box, or plastic sweater box has been converted into a serviceable terrarium, American hobbyists usually opt for the bare minimum—the absolute necessities if you will—when designing cages. Many hobbyists opt for little more than an absorbent substrate of folded newspaper, paper towels, or aspen shavings; an untippable water bowl; a hide box; and an escape-proof top. Fortunately, corn snakes thrive and breed in such spartan quarters.

Plastic shoe, sweater, and blanket boxes are available in many hardware and department stores. Purchase the type that comes with snap-on lids that will hold your snakes securely. Aquariums, of course, are available in virtually any pet store. Most of the same

stores will have easily secured tops in stock. Since corn snakes are not persistent climbers, all caging should be oriented in a normal horizontal position.

A corn snake cage need only be large enough to house the snakes comfortably. One or two hatchlings would be comfortable in a plastic shoe box-sized cage. A corn snake 14–24 inches (36–61 cm.) long needs a ten gallon (38 l) aquarium; an adult needs a 15–20 gallon (57–76 l) aquarium or a double shoe box-sized cage.

Ventilation is important. A wide variety of screen tops are available to fit any aquarium. If you use plastic caging, sufficient air (ventilation) holes must be drilled (or melted) through the sides to provide adequate air transfer and to prevent excessive humidity from building up within. Ventilation should be provided on at least two sides; three sides is better.

Racks specifically built to hold a dozen or more plastic boxes are now available. Many of these shelving units even have a heat tape built in. Most reptile magazines and many of the reptile expos now held across the country advertise these.

Very attractive and secure terraria, called lizard lounges and similar names, are now commercially available in several sizes. These make excellent enclosures for corn snakes.

The Cage

Limbs

Although corn snakes can climb, they do not persistently do so. They are more apt to climb just to the top of a fallen trunk than to ascend higher to the topmost branches of a standing tree. If you provide your corn snake with a climbing branch, the limb should be at least one-and-a-half times the diameter of the snake's body and securely propped in place.

Hide Boxes

Corn snakes are secretive in nature and prefer to be so in captivity. Captives should be provided with a hiding box, a cave, or some niche that provides seclusion and security. Several sizes and styles of preformed plastic caves are available from pet and reptile dealers. Even a cardboard box (like a shoe box) with an access hole cut in one end will suffice. Snakes like to have their coils in contact with the sides and also seem to prefer to have their back lightly touching the top of their hiding area. In other words, bigger is not always better. Suitably sized hollow limbs, found on woodland rambles, are also well accepted by the snakes but are harder to keep clean. Arches or tubes of cork bark (also available from many pet stores) are pretty, inexpensive, and easily sterilized when necessary.

Water, Soaking Bowls, and Cage Humidity

Although corn snakes are very tolerant of humidity extremes, cage humidity should be an important consideration. If humidity remains too low for an extended period, corn snakes may have shedding problems. If humidity remains so high that the terrarium is actually damp, serious skin problems such as blister disease can occur.

The size and placement of a water bowl can play an integral part in raising or lowering the humidity in a cage. Cage humidity will be higher in

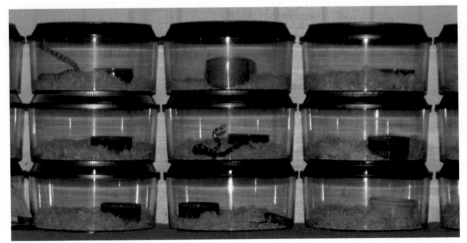

Because they are small and escape artists, hatchling corn snakes may be maintained in small but tightly covered cages.

Racks for translucent plastic boxes of various sizes are commercially available.

a cage with reduced ventilation than in one with greater air circulation. It will also be higher if you provide a large water bowl. If you wish to increase or retain a high humidity in your cage, place the water bowl onto the hottest spot (over a heating pad if the latter is in use). If you wish to decrease or keep humidity as low as possible, situate the water bowl onto the coolest spot in the cage.

A snake preparing to shed its skin may wish to soak in a large dish of tepid water. Seeking extra moisture at this time is natural, and you should allow it.

Lighting and Heating

Corn snakes, like all snakes, are ectothermic. They regulate their body temperatures to the correct parameters by utilizing outside sources of heating and cooling. At times, corn snakes may bask while fully exposed. At other times, such as when their vision is impaired by pending ecdysis or skin shedding, they may thermoregulate while remaining under cover. At times such as this, the snakes favor their hide box or, if in the wild, crawl under easily warmed items such as discarded sheets of plywood, rusted roofing tins, or flat rocks.

It is as important for snakes to remain comfortably cool as it is for them to remain comfortably warm. During heat waves or where temperatures are naturally very hot, corn snakes become primarily nocturnal in their activity patterns. Corn snakes are often most active during the dark of the moon and during periods of unsettled weather.

Natural light cycles are nearly as important to the snakes as temperature. Under normal conditions, corn snakes are most active during the lengthening days of spring and the long days of summer. These, of course, coincide with the most optimum temperatures as well. Those snakes that hibernate do so during the shortest days of the year. Even if kept warm in captivity, snakes may become lethargic and sporadic feeders as photoperiods wane in the autumn.

Snakes retain the need to thermoregulate even when captive. They, of course, then depend on us, their keepers, to provide them with the necessary parameters. Heating pads, heating tapes, and hot rocks (these latter not particularly recommended) can be used as contact heating sources. Both ceramic heating units that screw into a light socket and lightbulbs (especially those with directed beams such as floodlights and spotlights) can be used as alternate sources of heat. These must be mounted in a position where the snake cannot coil next

to them and get burned. The various lightbulbs, of course, also supply light. Fluorescent bulbs will provide light but little heat.

Is full-spectrum lighting necessary? No, it does not seem so. However, since not all aspects of snake behavior are yet understood, supplying as natural an environment as possible seems prudent.

Thermal Gradients

Except during hibernation when the terrarium temperature should be uniformly cool, thermal gradients should be provided. Keep one end of the tank cool (preferably 70–80°F [21–27°C]), and allow the other end to sit atop a heating unit of some type. Corn snakes will want the hot end in the 88–95°F (31–35°C) range. A hide box should be kept on the cool end of the tank or, if the tank is large enough, you may place one at both ends.

If the heating unit you choose is not thermostatically controlled, add an in-line rheostat or other such regulating device. Please note that while the current genre of heat rocks is more reliable than their predecessors, serious thermal burns have occurred during the use of these. If you choose to use a heat rock, monitor it very carefully.

Rather than heat/cool/light individual cages, some very successful hobbyists treat large collections of corn snakes, even if individually caged, as a single unit. The temperature of the room devoted to the collection is thermostatically controlled. The lighting, which usually coincides with a natural/normal photoperiod, is on a timer.

A 10-gallon terrarium with a sliding lockable top

Critter cages having tight-fitting and lockable sliding screened tops are available in many standard aquarium sizes. Unlike the plastic boxes, aquarium-style caging allows excellent visibility of your pets.

Feeding

In the wild, baby corn snakes often feed primarily on tree frogs and lizards. They also usually accept nestling rodents. A lizard diet seems especially ingrained in corn snakes from the Florida Keys or in other habitats where lizards may be more easily obtained than rodents. As babies, these snakes may not accept rodents until they reach several months of age. Lizards may remain a major component of the diet of these snakes well into adulthood. Corn snakes that eat primarily or exclusively a diet of lizards grow far more slowly and remain smaller than those that incorporate rodents into their diet.

The size of the food animal is tied to the size of the corn snake. Offer your hatchlings pinky mice, offer yearling corn snakes jumper mice or small adults, and offer corn snakes that are almost at the adult length adult mice. Once in a while, a small corn snake, especially if it is very hungry, will manage to consume a mouse that is far larger than the snake would normally tackle. However, a snake often regurgitates these too-big meals.

Whether you feed prekilled mice or live mice is your decision. Corn snakes do not need to kill their food in order to feed. Generation after generation have fed exclusively on prekilled mice simply because providing prekilled mice is much easier than maintaining a mouse colony.

Feeding prekilled mice is better because doing so is easier on the snake and, in an odd fashion, easier on the mouse. Prekilled mice are killed humanely and quickly. A prekilled mouse is not going to turn on its predator and bite out its eye or bite through its jaw. The risks taken with offering live food greatly increase if the mouse is left in with the snake overnight. Never do this.

If your snake has been feeding on lizards or tree frogs, you can wean it to rodents by scenting the pinky with a lizard or a tree frog. We have used frozen lizards and tree frogs with a great deal of success. Simply rub the thawed food item with the frozen lizard or tree frog. Concentrate mostly around the face of the pinky, the part the snake will take into its mouth first. Obviously, one lizard or tree frog will last a long time; just make sure it does not dry out too much in your freezer.

How Often to Feed

Feed adult corn snakes weekly. Each adult may eat from one to five

A leopard rat snake eats a prekilled mouse.

prekilled, thawed mice, depending on the size of the snake and the size of the mice. During the winter months, even though cage temperatures may not drop all that much, captive corn snakes will go off their feed and may not eat for a week or two at a time. In colder regions, corn snakes may go a month or longer during the winter months without feeding.

Assisted Feeding

If your corn snake refuses to feed for more than a month during warm weather, you may need to persuade it to eat. Since this type of feeding or any type of force-feeding is more traumatic for a snake than simply snacking on a mouse, you will need to use a smaller, more easily digested pinky mouse or a jumper.

Hold the snake by its head in one hand, and wind the snake's body around your arm to offer support.

Hold the pinky (thawed in hot water and blotted dry if it is frozen—never thaw it in a microwave) in your other hand, and gently work the nose of the pinky into the snake's mouth. As soon as you have the pinky's snout in the snake's mouth, put the snake into its cage, replace the cage lid, cover the cage with a towel or a sheet, and leave the room. The snake is more likely to continue swallowing the pinky if you leave it undisturbed.

Before Hibernation

If you decide to hibernate your snake, do not feed it for at least two weeks before the snake goes into hibernation. During hibernation, digestion stops almost entirely. Food left in the snake's stomach can cause serious problems (see the chapter on breeding for more information about hibernation).

Health

Generally, when healthy, corn snakes are very easy to keep. However, ascertaining good health is not always easy. Corn snakes, like other reptiles, may show no outward signs of ill health until a health problem is well advanced. Sometimes, normal behavior may lead a new hobbyist to think his or her snake might be ill. Here are some characteristic attributes of healthy corn snakes.

1. Corn snakes are secretive snakes. It is normal for them to remain coiled for long periods—sometimes for days—beneath cover. This characteristic in no way denotes ill health.

2. Corn snakes often lie quietly even when alert and hungry. They are wait-and-ambush predators, a hunting technique that requires little movement on the part of the snake. However, a hungry snake is more apt to move about in its cage than a sated one. A corn snake may be more active during barometric changes that herald an approaching frontal system.

3. When choosing your corn snake, look at its overall size and body weight. The snake should have neither longitudinal folds of skin on its body nor apparent ribs. A skin fold or accordion ribs indicate an unnatural thinness that may be associated with nonfeeding, dehydration, or other problems. Reversing this problem may not be possible. Ask whether the specimen in which you are interested is feeding, whether it has been sneezing, and if the snake is easily handled. Watch it feed if possible.

4. The snake should not be wheezing or sneezing. Wheezing and/or repeated sneezing can indicate that the snake has a respiratory ailment (usually a cold or pneumonia). Because snakes possess only a single functional lung, any ailment that creates even moderate respiratory distress is of extreme seriousness. An occasional sneeze is as natural to a snake as it is to us.

5. The snake should have no exudate from its nostrils or mouth. Exudate near the nostrils or around the mouth may indicate a respiratory problem or mouth rot.

Reptile veterinary medicine is a specialized field. Not every veterinarian is qualified or interested in reptile medicine. You should find a qualified veterinarian before you need the services of one.

6. The snake's throat should not be puffy, pulsing, or distended. A distended (puffy) or pulsing throat also indicates respiratory distress.

7. The snake should have no caseous (cheesy) material on its lips, gums, or elsewhere in the mouth. Mouth rot is characterized by caseous material on the gums, in the throat, in the openings of the nares, and around the glottis.

8. The snake should have no open wounds. A number of factors may cause open wounds or patches of withered or discolored scales. Among these are cuts, burns, or the early removal, improper removal, or nonremoval of a skin that should have been shed. No matter the cause, do not purchase this snake.

9. The corn snake should not have a kinked or ankylosed spine. Improper incubation temperatures, physical injury, or genetic problems may cause spinal kinking (scoliosis) or fusing (ankylosis). The malformed spine may be just a visually distressing malformation, or it may be an outward manifestation of internal malformations.

10. When you lift it, the corn snake should not hang limply. Disease or advanced starvation may cause lack of muscle tone or weakness. Rehabilitation of a snake such as this is difficult, time consuming, or impossible. Again, do not purchase this snake.

11. The snake should not have any ectoparasites (ticks or mites). Although these are dealt with fairly easily, they are evidence of poor hygiene on the current keeper's part.

12. The snake should not have any remnants of unshed skin remaining. Unshed skins result from improper husbandry. Most may be attributed to improper humidity/moisture levels in the corn snake's cage. Ill health, including acute dehydration, can also cause it.

The Shedding Process

How frequently should a corn snake shed its skin? The growth rate and overall health of your corn snake will have much to do with the frequency with which it sheds its skin. A healthy, fast-growing baby will shed two or three times more frequently than a slowly growing adult or an ill specimen. However, a specimen suffering from blister disease (white bubbles on the skin, usually caused by overly damp or unclean quarters) will usually

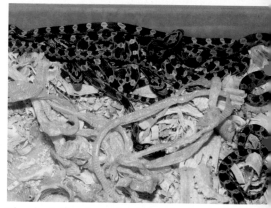

The shed skins (post-hatching shed) are easily visible here. As they grow, snakes continue to shed periodically throughout their lives.

enter a rapid shed cycle no matter its age. If the cause of the blistering is corrected, all evidence of the disease will often disappear after two or three sheds. Corn snakes also typically shed following emergence from hibernation. Females shed several days prior to egg deposition. The hatchlings shed a few days after hatching. Adult corn snakes shed about three or four times a year.

The shedding process (also called molting or, more properly, ecdysis) results from thyroid activity. A week or so prior to shedding, a suffusion of lymph loosens old skin from the new one forming beneath it. Your corn snake may take on an overall grayish or silvery sheen. Even its eyes will temporarily look bluish. This is the phase of the shedding cycle colloquially referred to as blue or opaque by hobbyists. A few days prior to shedding, your corn snake's eyes will clear and the pattern will again become moderately bright. However, not until after the actual shedding has occurred will the snake will be at its colorful best.

Although in the wild snakes seldom have problems shedding, some captives may. The process itself takes less than half an hour. To start, the snake rubs its nose on a log or rock in its enclosure to loosen the skin around the lips. It then merely crawls forward, everting and leaving the old skin behind. Shedding problems may often be associated with specimens newly collected from the wild, specimens that are dehydrated or in otherwise suboptimal conditions, or when the relative humidity in the terrarium or cage is too low. Examine the shed skin to make sure that the eye caps have been shed. Even when shedding is otherwise successful, the old skin

may adhere to the tail tip or to the eyes. If these pieces are not manually (and very carefully) removed by the keeper, they can restrict circulation. This can result in the loss of the tail tip or, if on the eyes, impaired vision and eventual blindness. If patches of shed skin adhere, a gentle misting with tepid water or a drop of mineral oil may help your snake rid itself of the pieces. A dab of mineral oil seems to work especially well when loosening adhering eye caps (brilles).

All exfoliating skin must be removed. If it does not come off easily, placing your corn snake into a damp cloth bag (make sure the temperature is suitable) and leaving it overnight may loosen the skin and allow your snake to shed. Placing some damp paper towels inside the dampened bag may be of even more assistance. Another technique is to confine the snake to a tepid water bath—which does not quite cover the snake—overnight. A rough branch will assist in shedding.

Occasionally, you may have to help your snake manually rid itself of a particularly resistant shed. Avoid a recurrence by assuring that your corn snake drinks sufficiently to remain fully hydrated and by increasing cage humidity.

Handling: Do's and Don'ts

Although most corn snakes will allow gentle handling, others may resist such familiarity at first. If your snake does bite you, do *not* yank your hand roughly from its mouth. If you do so, you are quite apt to break the teeth and injure the gums of your snake.

Such injuries may result in mouth rot (infectious stomatitis), which can be difficult to cure and fatal if not treated.

Do not drop your snake. A drop can result in damage to internal organs or other injury. This is especially true if your snake is gravid. Although an occasionally arboreal species like the corn snake may be a little more accustomed to an occasional fall, they still should never be handled carelessly.

Quarantine

To prevent the spread of diseases and parasites between snakes, you should quarantine new specimens for a given period of time. A month seems best, but even a week would be better than no quarantine at all. During quarantine, frequent behavioral observations and other tests should be run to determine the readiness of placing the new specimen with those already being maintained. During this time, fecal exams should be carried out to determine whether or not endoparasites are present. For this, seek the expertise of a qualified reptile veterinarian. The quarantine area should be completely removed from the area in which other reptiles are kept, preferably in another room.

You should thoroughly clean the quarantine tank prior to introducing the new snake(s). Regularly clean it throughout the quarantine period. As with any other terrarium, the quarantine tank should be geared to the needs of your corn snake. You must take into consideration temperature, humidity, size, lighting, and all other factors.

In an attempt to escape or to find food, wild-collected, nervous, or hungry corn snakes may abrade their rostral scale in an attempt to escape. They are less apt to do this if a hiding place is provided.

Only after you (and your veterinarian) are completely satisfied that your new specimen(s) are healthy and habituated should they be brought near other specimens. This quarantine period can be one of the most important periods in the life of your corn snake. The importance of quarantine should not be overlooked and cannot be overemphasized!

Stress

Just as stress can cause problems in higher animals, it can also be debilitating in reptiles. Wild-collected corn snakes are often more prone to stress-related problems than those that are captive bred. The collecting, the shipping, the caging—all are stressful to a degree, and the stress is something that you must strive to eliminate. Providing a secure artificial habitat—a hide box, perches, an adequate substrate, water, and food—and keeping the corn snake's cage in a low-traffic area are all a part of stress elimination. Doing all you can to reduce stress in

captivity will help your corn snakes live their expected 20-years-plus life span.

Burns, Bites, and Abscesses

Prevention of these three problems is not difficult and requires just a little forethought on the part of the keeper. Covering incandescent lightbulbs and fixtures and ascertaining that the surface of your hot rocks or blocks do not go above 95°F (35°C) will eliminate the burn problem. If, by accident, your snake is burned, cool the burned area, and apply a clean dressing until you take the snake to your vet.

An improperly sterilized and healed burn or bite may result in the formation of an abscess. Some abscesses will eventually heal and slough off or be rubbed off; a very few may require surgical removal. Consult your reptile veterinarian.

Respiratory Ailments

Because they have only a single functional lung, a snake's respiratory problems must be immediately identified and just as immediately corrected. Treatments that effectively combat some respiratory ailments are not necessarily equally effective against all. Likewise, a medication that works effectively on one species of snake might well not work well on another. Some aminoglycoside drugs that are ideally suited for curing a given respiratory problem may be so nephrotoxic that they kill the snake if the animal is dehydrated in the least. Some respiratory ailments are resistant to the old cadre of treatments—ampicillin, amoxicillin, tetracycline, or penicillin. Thus, with all of these variables in mind and the probable seriousness of the problem if the respiratory ailment worsens, we feel it is mandatory that at the first sign of respiratory distress, you seek the advice of a qualified reptile veterinarian. Do not let the bubbling, wheezing, and rasping continue. You can help by elevating the cage temperature and maintaining normal humidity. Since some respiratory diseases are communicable, quarantine the sick snake in a separate cage, preferably in a separate room.

Infectious Stomatitis (Mouth Rot)

Sulfa drugs have long been the medication of choice for treating mouth rot. Treatment options have changed, and many new pharmaceuticals are now available. Please consult your reptile veterinarian for her or his recommendation.

Blister Disease

Although this is usually a malady associated with dirty water and unclean quarters, blister disease sometimes crops up when the humidity in a cage is overly high or when the substrate becomes wet. First and foremost, correct the cause. Lower the cage humidity, sterilize the cage, and provide new, dryer substrate. If the blister disease is minimal, your snake will probably enter a rapid shed cycle and divest itself of the problems

within a shed or two. If the disease is advanced and has caused underlying tissue to become necrotic, you must rupture each blister and clean the area daily (for 7 to 14 days) with dilute Betadyne and/or hydrogen peroxide. Again, your snake will enter a rapid shed cycle. After two sheds, its skin should appear normal. This can be a fatal disease if not caught and treated promptly.

Ectoparasites: Ticks and Mites

You can spot-spray a tick with a commercial reptile ivermectin spray and wait for the tick to die, or you can remove the tick using a pair of tick-removal tweezers (used for dogs and available online and in pet stores, feed stores, and some hardware stores). The tick tweezers look like a cheap plastic gadget, but they work by grasping the tick by its head, not by its body. The tweezers are then rotated—no real pulling or squeezing of the tick's body is involved—and the tick is essentially unscrewed from your snake's flesh. Crush the tick and dispose of the remains.

On snakes, mites are more commonly encountered (and more difficult to eradicate!) than ticks. Mites not only transfer easily from cage to cage but carry and spread diseases as well. Unlike ticks, which occur singly, mites are usually present in immense numbers. You need to treat the snake and its caging. While doing so, use an easily cleaned and readily replaceable substrate such as newspaper or paper towels (for the time being, no mulch, no wood shavings, and no leaves) in each cage. If you have multiple cages

sterilize your hands between cages; mites are easily transported from cage to cage. Mite eggs hatch every nine days, so your treatment will have to be repeated in nine days to kill the new emergents.

Use a commercial reptile ivermectin mite spray, being very careful not to get the spray in your snake's eyes or mouth, and spray the stripped caging as well. Put in new substrate, a scrubbed hide box, a well-washed water dish, and thoroughly cleaned (or new) rocks, branches, and other cage furniture. Do not use any sort of multi-layer substrate during the mite treatment process.

Repeat the spray and cage cleaning in nine days. If this doesn't take care of your mite problem, your best bet at this point is to take your snake to your reptile veterinarian for injectable ivermectin. The treatment must be repeated in nine days to kill the hatchling mites.

Internal Parasites

When pet corn snakes were collected from the wild, endoparasites (such as protozoans, amoebae, trichomonads, coccidia, cestodes, trematodes, and nematodes) were fairly common. Now that the vast majority of corn snakes are captive bred and captive hatched (cb/ch), endoparasites and the problems they cause are seldom encountered. When you suspect endoparasites could be present, your reptile veterinarian is your best choice. New, very effective treatments are available and most are affordable. Your veterinarian will be able to provide you with safe dosages and suggestions for newer choices.

Breeding

When the first corn snakes were bred in captivity, it opened the doors to a new dimension of snake keeping: the providing of captive-bred snakes to a growing market of snake hobbyists. This was quite a breakthrough, and one that conservationists, breeders, and hobbyists warmly endorsed.

The corn snake proved the ideal subject, both as a pet and as a breeding snake. Since the snakes were quite variable in coloration, both geographically and within localized populations, hobbyists might be persuaded to keep more than a single corn snake.

Today, tens of thousands of baby corn snakes are produced annually in captive collections. Breeding corn snakes is not a difficult process. All you need are corn snakes of the opposite sex and a few caging modifications.

How to Sex Your Corn Snake

Despite their general similarity of appearance, male and female corn snakes do differ somewhat in size, build, and, especially (if the corn snake is sexually mature), tail shape and comparative length. Males do tend to be the larger sex (sometimes considerably so). Except when females are gravid, the males are also the more robust in build.

Three definitive ways exist to sex your corn snake. These three methods include comparing the shape and length of the tail (of sexually mature snakes), probing (any size snakes), and popping the hemipenes (in hatchling snakes). Since the latter two methods can injure your snakes if done incorrectly, we strongly urge that you learn these techniques from an experienced herper.

The comparative shape and length of your corn snake's tail is most obvious if you check it from the underside. To begin with, males have proportionately longer tails. The copulatory organs of a male snake

The tip of a nose is barely visible in this just-hatching clutch of eggs.

(called hemipenes) are hollow sheaths that, when retracted, are housed in the tail base. Because of this, the tail of a sexually mature adult male corn snake is quite broad at the vent and for about ten scale-lengths thereafter. Then it tapers rather evenly for its remaining length. The tail of an adult female corn snake is narrower at the vent. Because it is shorter, a female's tail tapers more abruptly.

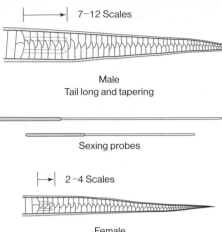

Male
Tail long and tapering

Sexing probes

Female
Tail short and abruptly tapered

Probing, if done carefully, is a definitive method of sexing corn snakes of any age. In males, a lubricated probe can be inserted distally for a distance of six or eight subcaudal scales (the scales beneath the tail). The probe is actually inserted into the cloaca and then into the retracted hemipenis and pushed gently to the tip. This must be carefully done. If the hemipenis is injured along its length or ruptured at the tip by using a probe of incorrect diameter or unwarranted pressure, future breeding capabilities will be diminished or curtailed. Females, of course, lack the hemipenes. The probe will reach distally only two or three subcaudal scale lengths in them.

The hemipenes of hatchling male corn snakes are easily everted by a process termed popping. Again, to prevent injury, this must be accomplished gently. To evert the hemipenes, the hatchling snake should be held belly up and its tail angled upward at the vent (anal opening). Your thumb should be placed about ten subcaudal scales toward the tip of the tail, beyond the anus. Press the ball of your thumb firmly against the snake's tail. Then roll your thumb forward. When done properly, the pressure of your thumb will evert the hemipenes of the male. The everted hemipenes are usually bright red in color. Although no hemipenes are present on females, a tiny spot of bright red often occurs at each side of the vent. The hemipenes will retract a few moments after the pressure on the tail is relieved. This technique is used only on newly hatched corn snakes or on those a month old at the most.

Cycling for Reproduction

Unlike other species of snakes, many corn snakes, especially those from the deep South, do not require hibernation to cycle reproductively. Additionally, after having been bred for several generations in captivity, even those corn snakes from more northerly latitudes seem to require less precise cycling methods than those snakes taken directly from the wild.

However, to attain their full breeding, captive corn snakes should be given at least a slight winter cooling as well as a corresponding reduction

A hatching amelanistic corn snake views its world.

in photoperiod. All you need to do is to provide a shortened day cycle, a daytime winter temperature of 75 to 83°F (24 to 28°C), and nighttime lows of 66 to 70°F (19 to 21°C) for about three months. During this period, the breeders can be sparingly fed. Since digestion is suboptimal, the meals should be small. Keep fresh drinking water in the cage.

If you choose to provide an actual hibernation period for your corn snake (and many hobbyists prefer to do so), withhold food for two weeks before the hibernation period. Put the corn snake into a ventilated shoe box with sphagnum or mulch substrate. Put the box (or the entire cage) into an area where the temperature will stay at 50 to 55°F (10 to 13°C) for a period of 90 days during hibernation. (Snakes hibernated at over 55°F (13°C) tend to lose too much body weight and may not survive the hibernation process.) Leave the water bowls in place, and check every two weeks to make sure the water is fresh.

Some breeders retain their snakes in total darkness during hibernation; others allow a natural winter photoperiod. Since we used a modified

refrigerator for our hibernaculum, the snakes were in total darkness except when we took them out at two-week intervals to check their well-being.

When the snakes are removed from hibernation at the end of the hibernation period, drinking/soaking water should be immediately available. The snakes will usually feed a few days after their cooling/hibernation. Feeding the snakes heavily once they have been warmed again is imperative. Females, especially, need ample body weight to fulfill their full breeding potential. Both males and females will shed their skin a week or two following their period of cooling/hibernation and will breed almost immediately thereafter.

After the winter cooling period, to breed your snakes, simply place the sexes together in a cage and make sure the temperature is 75 to 85°F (24 to 29°C). Lightly misting the cage may help. Reproductive behavior is often stimulated by the lowering barometric pressures that occur at the advent of a spring (more rarely an autumn) storm or by misting. The male should show an active interest in the female. Both sexes should demonstrate very active tongue flickering. The male will bring his body alongside the female's, and the two will bring their tails into juxtaposition. The male will flip the tip of his tail over the female's and insert his hemipenis into her cloaca to inseminate her. They may breed repeatedly, but usually one breeding is enough to impregnate the female.

The female will begin to put on weight and will appear fatter about 45 days after breeding. During this time, she may avail herself of a warm, secure basking area. She lays eggs some 60 days after mating, usually in April or

May. Egg count may vary from 5 to 30 eggs, depending on the age and condition of the snake. The female will stop feeding about three weeks before egg deposition and will shed a week before deposition. Both the cessation of feeding and the shed are signals for you to provide an egg deposition site. During this time, avoid rapid cage temperature changes and handling the female more than necessary. Excessive or rough handling of a gestating female and/or an improper cage temperature may result in the deposition of inviable eggs or stillborn young.

An opaque plastic tub partially filled with barely moistened peat or sphagnum will often be accepted by a gravid female as a deposition tub. This becomes even more desirable to the snake if it is darkened by placing the tub inside a darkened cardboard box. Be sure that an appropriately sized entrance hole is easily accessible. If the cage temperature is inordinately cold, you can set the deposition tub on top of a heating cable or pad (set on low) to increase warmth. Remember that heat from beneath will quickly dry the sphagnum (or other medium), and remoistening will be necessary on a regular basis. If eggs have already been laid, take care not to wet them directly when remoistening the medium in the deposition tub.

Incubation and Incubators— Commercial or Home Made?

Although its beauty and genetic plasticity may be the corn snake's principal claim to fame, its fecundity and the ease with which the eggs of this species can be incubated and hatched are close secondary draws.

Although healthy adult female captive corn snakes normally double-clutch, some females are known to have produced three and (rarely) even four clutches during a given breeding season. A female that has double or triple-clutched may need supplementary calcium.

Corn snake eggs require only a bit of moisture in a clean substrate, a fairly high ambient humidity, darkness, and a temperature that hovers close to 81°F. Although a constant incubation temperature is the best, slow fluctuations between 78 and 83°F will not harm corn snake eggs.

Sustained temperatures below 78°F or above 83°F may result in skeletal deformities of the developing embryos or in egg death. Excessive heat can be every bit as detrimental to the developing eggs as excessively cool temperatures.

Although some hobbyists choose to incubate corn snake eggs at room temperature (78–83°F), volume breed-

Clutches may contain from only a few to more than 20 eggs.

Build Your Own Incubator

Materials needed: styrofoam cooler (you choose the size); thermostat (this must not be preset for bird-hatching temperatures), either wafer (inexpensive) or solid-state (such as Spyder Robotics; expensive but very reliable); instruction book that accompanies each thermostat (incorrectly attaching electrical wiring connections can disable or destroy the thermostat or cause fire or injury, so follow the wiring diagram exactly!); heating unit (coil, cable, or other [Flexwatt heat tape is a good choice]); electric cord (including wall plug and connector for heating unit); thermometer; wire nuts or connectors; a plastic or wire shelf; 4 evenly cut 1½-inch lengths of 2-inch-diameter PVC to hold the shelf above the heating unit and bottom of the incubator.

Because the protruding rheostat controls the wafers themselves, a wafer thermostat must be placed on the top or the side of the incubator. This can be very inconvenient. Poke a hole through the lid of the Styrofoam cooler so you can suspend the thermostat/heater inside the box. Add another hole for a thermometer so you can check on the inside temperature without opening the top. If the thermometer does not have a flange to keep it from slipping through the hole in the lid, use a rubber band wound several times around the thermometer to form a flange.

Poke another hole through the lower side of the cooler. Pull the heat tape through the hole, leaving the plug end out. Arrange

ers usually prefer the comparative security and stability of an incubator. Incubators may be purchased commercially or be homemade.

The price for reliable commercial incubators begins at about $150 and tops out in the several thousands of dollars. There are a few models that sell for $100 or less, but temperature/humidity control may not be as exact as you would like. The cost of the materials needed to build your own

the heat tape into a continuous series of loops across the bottom of the cooler. Cut off the distal end, and splice the tape to the thermostat with the wire nuts.

Put the lid onto the cooler, and plug in the thermostat/heater. Wait half an hour, and check the temperature. The L-pin handle on the top of the thermostat is the rheostat. Adjust the thermostat/heater until the temperature inside the incubator is within the desired range.

Once the temperature is regulated, put the container of eggs inside the incubator on the wire shelf and close the lid. Check the temperature daily, and adjust as needed. The preferred humidity is near 100 percent. Keep the hatching medium moist by adding water if needed. Use a nonventilated container and keep the hatching medium damp to the touch but too dry to be able to squeeze out any water by hand.

By the end of the first week, infertile eggs will turn yellow, harden, and begin to collapse. Remove them. At the end of the incubation period—which usually lasts 60 to 70 days—the baby corn snakes will cut a slit in their eggs with an egg tooth on the tip of their snouts.

The babies do not seem eager to leave the eggs. They will cut a slit, look out, and decide to stay inside the eggs for a while longer, perhaps as long as a day and a half. Those that leave the eggs can be removed to another terrarium and offered food, a sunning spot, and water. They should shed within a few days.

incubator would be almost the same. The choice is yours. All models will hold several clutches of corn snake eggs.

Corn snake hatchlings rarely have difficulty emerging from their eggs when incubation parameters are correct. In very unusual cases, the babies may need just a little help. Elevating the relative humidity in the incubator may help.

Glossary

Albino: Lacking black pigment.

Allele: One of a pair of alternative Mendelian characteristics. A gene.

Allopatric: Not occurring together but often occurring adjacently.

Ambient temperature: The temperature of the surrounding environment.

Amelanistic: Lacking black pigment; albino.

Anal plate: Large scute (or scutes) covering the snake's anus.

Anerythristic: Lacking red pigment.

Anterior: Toward the front.

Anus: The external opening of the cloaca; the vent.

Arboreal: Tree dwelling.

Axanthic: Lacking yellow pigment.

Brille: The transparent spectacle covering the eyes of a snake.

Caudal: Pertaining to the tail.

cb/cb: Captive bred, captive born.

cb/ch: Captive bred, captive hatched.

Cloaca: The common chamber into which digestive, urinary, and reproductive systems empty and that itself opens exteriorly through the vent or anus.

Constricting: To wrap tightly in coils and squeeze.

Crepuscular: Active at dusk and/or dawn.

Deposition: As used here, the laying of the eggs.

Deposition site: The spot chosen by the female to lay her eggs.

Diploid: Having two sets of chromosomes.

Diurnal: Active in the daytime.

Dominance: The ability of one of a pair of alleles to suppress the expression of the other.

Dorsal: Pertaining to the back; upper surface.

Dorsolateral: Pertaining to the upper sides.

Dorsum: The upper surface.

Double recessive: Containing two recessive characteristics that would be masked by a dominant gene; homozygous recessive.

Ecological niche: The precise habitat utilized by a species.

Ectothermic: Cold-blooded.

Endothermic: Warm-blooded.

Erythristic: A prevalence of red pigment.

F1: First generation.

F2: Second generation; the result of breeding a pair of F1s.

Form: An identifiable species or subspecies.

Gametes: Egg cells and sperm cells.

Gene: One transmitter of hereditary characters.

Genus: A taxonomic classification of a group of species having similar characteristics. The genus falls between the next higher designation of family and the next lower designation of species. It is always capitalized when written. Genera is the plural of genus.

Gravid: The reptilian equivalent of mammalian pregnancy.

Gular: Pertaining to the throat.

Haploid: Containing a single copy of each chromosome.

Heliothermic: Pertaining to a species that basks in the sun to thermoregulate.

Hemipenes: The dual copulatory organs of male corn snakes.

Hemipenis: The singular form of hemipenes.

Herpetoculture: The captive breeding of reptiles and amphibians.

Herpetoculturist: One who indulges in herpetoculture.

Herpetologist: One who indulges in herpetology.

Herpetology: The study (often scientifically oriented) of reptiles and amphibians.

Heterozygous: Having two differing copies of a particular gene.

Hibernacula: Winter dens.

Homozygous: Having two like copies of a particular gene.

Hybrid: Offspring resulting from the breeding of two different species.

Hydrate: To restore body moisture by drinking or absorption.

Insular: Of or pertaining to an island.

Intergrade: Offspring resulting from the breeding of two subspecies.

Jacobson's organs: Highly enervated olfactory pits in the palate of snakes and lizards.

Juvenile: A young or immature specimen.

Keel: A ridge (along the center of a scale).

Labial: Pertaining to the lips.

Lateral: Pertaining to the sides.

Melanistic: A profusion of black pigment.

Middorsal: Pertaining to the middle of the back.

Midventral: Pertaining to the center of the belly or abdomen.

Nocturnal: Active at night.

Ontogenetic: Age-related (color) changes.

Oviparous: Reproducing by means of eggs that hatch after laying.

Photoperiod: The daily/seasonally variable length of the hours of daylight.

Race: A subspecies.

Recessive: As used here, a gene masked by a dominant allele.

Scenting: A technique used to encourage reluctant feeders. A pinky or larger mouse is rubbed with a prey item the snake likes, such as a lizard. Usually, this needs to be done only a few times until the snake will eat unscented prey items on its own.

Scute: Scale.

Species: A group of similar creatures that produce viable young when bred. This taxonomic designation falls beneath genus and above subspecies. Abbreviation: sp.

Subcaudal: Beneath the tail.

Subspecies: The subdivision of a species. A race that may differ slightly in color, size, scales, or other criteria. Abbreviation: ssp.

Sympatric: Occurring together.

Taxonomy: The science of classifying plants and animals.

Terrestrial: Land dwelling.

Thermoregulate: To regulate (body) temperature by choosing a warmer or cooler environment.

Thigmothermic: Pertaining to a species (often nocturnal) that thermoregulates against a warmed substrate.

Vent: The external opening of the cloaca; the anus.

Venter: The underside of a creature; the belly.

Ventral: Pertaining to the undersurface or belly.

Ventrolateral: Pertaining to the sides of the venter.

Helpful Information

Professional herpetological societies publish periodicals and monographs about various aspects of herpetology and the biology of many reptiles and amphibians. Two such societies are

Society for the Study of Amphibians and
  Reptiles
Dept. of Zoology
Miami University
Oxford, OH 45056

Herpetologist's League
c/o Texas Nat. Heritage Program
Texas Parks and Wildlife Dept.
4200 Smith School Rd.
Austin, TX 78744

Two technical publications are *Copeia* and *Herpetologica*.

Fellow amateurs and professionals may also be found at the biology departments of museums, universities, high schools, and nature centers. Many larger cities have herpetological societies, naturalists' clubs, or zoos.

There is one major hobbyist magazine.

Reptiles
P. O. Box 6050
Mission Viejo, CA 92690

To find a good source of information and to contact fellow hobbyists, use on-line services. Three places to start (which contain many links) include *reptilesonline.com*, *animalnetwork.com/ reptiles/web/default.asp*, and *kingsnake.com*.

Index

Breeding, 38–43
Burns, bites, and
  abscesses, 35
Caging, 26–28
  Accessories, 27–28
  Temperatures, 28
Collecting, 11
Colors,
  Albino, 20
  Amelanistic, 15, 20
  Anerythristic, 18
  Aztec, 24–25
  Blizzard, 23
  Blood red, 22
  Butter, 24
  Candy cane, 22
  Caramel, 23
  Chocolate, 21
  Christmas, 23
  Creamsicle, 25
  Florida Keys, 20–21
  Ghost, 23
  Hypomelanistic, 23

Melanistic
  (See Anerythristic)
Lavender, 23
Miami, 17
Milk, 25
Motley, 25
Normal, 16
Okeetee, 16, 19, 23
Olive, 21
Orange, 21
Pepper, 23–24
Snow, 22
Striped, 22, 24
Sunglow, 20
Red albino, 20
Rosy, 3
Type A amelanistic, 19
Type B amelanistic, 19
White albino, 20
Cooling, 40
Eggs, 40–41
*Elaphe guttata,
  emoryi*, 3

rosacea, 3
Feeding, 4, 30–31
Great Plains rat snake, 3,
  25
Handling, 12, 34–35
Health, 32–37
Hibernation, 31, 40
Illness, symptoms, 36–37
Incubation, 41–43
Infectious stomatitus
  (mouth rot), 36
Medications, 37
Ordering and shipping,
  12–13
Parasites,
  Ticks and mites, 37
  Internal, 37
Range, 2
Respiratory ailments, 36
Shedding, 33–34
Sexing, 38–39
Size, 4
Temperature, 29, 40–41